T0128645

Saturday Mornings
WITH
Grandma
Theresa King's Recipes

TERI WATKINS

AuthorHouse™
1663 Liberty Drive
Bloomington, IN 47403
www.authorhouse.com
Phone: 833-262-8899

Special Thanks to Megan Schindele for editorial assistance, Andy Mays and Erica Knuth for assistance with
photos, and Declan Griner for finding the easiest way to type what seemed like millions of fractions.

Permission for back cover image provided by St. John's Catholic Church, Lincoln Nebraska

Author Photo by Cherri Dupree

ISBN: 978-1-6655-2320-2 (sc)
978-1-6655-2321-9 (e)

Library of Congress Control Number: 2021908933

Published by AuthorHouse 05/05/2021

authorHOUSE®

Table of Contents

Theresa (tallest) and her siblings.

Dick and Theresa King

Caption: (l-r) Stacy Watkins Lawson, Remer Griner, Hugh Lawson,
Grandma Theresa, Amy Watkins Griner. Probably Christmas 1990

Introduction

Theresa Marie Venuta King, my maternal grandmother, was born on August 17, 1910. She was raised in the gold-mining town of Lead, South Dakota. One day, she met a nice man working on roads for a utility company, and after a short courtship, with her family's blessing; she married Richard Edwin King from Ault, Colorado on July 5th, 1929.

Shortly after the wedding, Richard—known as Dick—was transferred to another location. According to the family story, their car broke down on the way in Lincoln Nebraska, and they were stuck with little money and no paycheck. After they decided to stay, they raised three children, Raymond, Larry, and Judy. Theresa worked and volunteered at the church, and Dick worked at the gas company, tended to their gardens, and went fishing when he could. Theresa was always cooking.

She told me once that during the war years and then after Dick was diagnosed with diabetes, it was just easier to cook at home. Even so, cooking became more difficult when her boys moved out and there were fewer people to feed. That was why she wanted family to visit, so that she could cook for them.

Some of my earliest memories involve our whole family, including my mom's brothers, gathering every week at Grandma and Grandpa's house on Saturday morning at 10:00 a.m. for our coffee. There was always a homemade treat—cookies or cakes or a gooey dessert. We would spend about an hour catching up with the week's news and then slowly wander off to do our errands.

I spent summers with my grandparents. As they raised all their own vegetables and strawberries, we would spend our mornings harvesting and our afternoons cooking. We had simple, delicious meals with fresh vegetables and meat and a nice dessert before bedtime.

These are her recipes, gathered from her recipe drawer and her and my mom's recipe boxes, as well as the ones I wrote down when I stayed with her. At one point, she had typed about one hundred recipes on index cards. However, mostly she used whatever piece of paper she found handy—the backs of envelopes, notepads from the local gas company that Grandpa brought home, birthday cards, or the backs of grocery or errand lists. Recipe cards are in her handwriting, and while I do not remember her kitchen ever being messy, the recipes are well used.

When I started typing these up in the summer of 2020, I decided to keep in them her style of writing. She abbreviated a lot but made very few typos. I have added a few comments here and there, but mostly these are just her recipes.

I hope you enjoy them!

Breads

Loaf of Bread

1¼ cups water
1 pkg yeast
2 TBS soft shortening
2 tsp salt
2 T sugar
3 cup flour

Dissolve the yeast in mixing bowl with water. Add shortening, salt, sugar, and half of the flour. Beat two minutes at min. speed with mixer, scrape the sides and bottom of bowl frequently, add remaining flour and blend with a spoon until smooth. Cover with a cloth, let rise in warm place for 30 minutes

Beat batter about 25 strokes, and spread evenly in greased bread pan. Smooth top and pat into shape with floured hand. Let rise, until dough is quarter inch from the top of the bowl, bake 45-50 minutes in 375° oven, til brown. Remove from pan, place on cooling rack to cool. Brush top with melted butter.

Banana Nut Bread

(large batch)
1 cup sugar
½ cup shortening (oleo)
2 eggs
3 good bananas, mashed
2½ cups flour
½ cup nuts
1 tsp baking soda

Dissolve soda in T of warm water. Mix in ingredients in order. Bake in 3 loaf pans 1 hour. 350°

Dumplings

sift 1 cup flour, 1 tsp salt, and ½ tsp baking powder, add ½ cup milk, and 2 TBS fat or salad oil to make soft dough.

Monkey Bread

2/3 cup sugar and 1 tsp cinnamon mixed together.

4 can's Pillsbury country style biscuits, quartered and rolled in sugar mixture and place in ungreased Bundt pan.

Melt 1½ cup butter or Marg. Mix with 1 cup sugar, 1 tsp cinnamon, and pour over biscuits. Bake at 350° for 45 minutes; let cool 15 minutes before turning out on plate. Can top with chopped nuts

Lemon Bread (on a card from the gas company)

½ cup shortening
¾ cup sugar
2 beaten eggs
1 ½ cups flour
1 tea. Baking powder
½ tea. salt
½ cup milk
grated rind of one lemon

Cream shortening and butter, add beaten eggs and beat together, Sift dry ingredients and add alternately with milk. Stir in grated lemon rind, and put into two loaf pans, Bake in gas oven at 350° for 50 minutes. Put glaze on in the pan while hot.

Glaze: Mix ½ cup sugar with juice of one Lemon, and pour over hot bread.

Kolaches

½ cup butter
½ cup lard
2 tsp salt
¾ cup sugar
5c fresh yeast*
3 cups scalded milk, cooled to lukewarm
4 egg yolks beaten well,
Enough Flour to make soft dough like biscuits

Combine fat, salt and sugar, dissolve yeast, in a little lukewarm milk and then all other ingredients. Let raise for double bulk, pinch it down, and let it rise again.

Form ball balls, and put on greased pans and let it rise again. Let rise to double the size. With finger, make depression in the center of each ball. Fill with cooked fruit such as prunes, apricots or poppy seed filling. Bake at 375° for ½ hour or until nicely browned.

*I cannot find what 5c might be for yeast. Most yeast packets are 5-7 grams. I would recommend that.

Oatmeal Muffins

1 cup sifted flour
2 teas baking powder
½ teas salt, soda, and cinnamon
1 cup quick cooking oatmeal
½ cup firm packed brown sugar
1 cup buttermilk
1 egg beaten
¼ cup cooking oil

Sift together flour, baking powders, salt, soda and cinnamon. Combine oats, brown sugar and buttermilk in separate bowl. Let stand 10 minutes, then add egg and oil, Add dry ingredients and mix to just moistened. Spoon batter into greased muffin pans, filing to 2/3 full. Bake at 375° for 20 minutes or done.

Quick Soda Bread

2 c sifted flour
2 TBL sugar
2 tsp baking powder
½ tsp salt
¼ tsp soda*
1 cup currants
1 cup buttermilk
Butter or Marg.
*assuming this is baking soda

Sift flour, sugar, b.power, salt and soda, stir in currants, then buttermilk til just blended. Turn out on floured board and knead 10 times. Shape into a 6 inch round on to a cookie sheet, ungreased. Cut cross on top. Bake in med oven at 375° 40 mins til golden, Brush top with butter or margarine. Break apart or slice to eat. Serve warm.

Note: to reheat, sprinkle with a few drops of water and wrap in clean paper bag or foil. Heat at 375° for 10-15 mins.

Popovers

Into a bowl break, 2 eggs add 1 c. milk. 1 cup sifted flour and ½ tsp salt

Mix with a spoon until eggs are well blended, disregard lumps, Fill 6 well-greased glass custard cups ¾ full. Set in muffin tin for easy handling. Place in cold oven. Set and light oven for 450°. Do not open oven for ½ hour. Popovers should be tall and buttery brown. Remove from over, puncture four sides of neck to let stem escape. Return to oven for 10 minutes with heat off to get crusty-delicious.
NOTE: to reheat these popovers simply place on cooky sheet without touching each other. Heat at 350° fir about 5 minutes.

Potato Rolls

1 cup mashed potatoes
1 cup potato water
⅔ c. sugar shortening
2 eggs beaten
⅓ cup sugar
1 pkg. yeast
1 tsp salt

Place mash and water in a bowl, Mix in the additional ingredients. Add enough flour to make soft dough. Work down, and rise double in bulk, work down again and make into rolls or you can place in refridge and keep until you want more rolls.

No baking instructions

Ravioli Dough

3 cups flour
3 eggs +2 yolks
4 T Oil
4 T water

Mix and roll in batches to fill. Cover with damp cloth when filling.

Cakes

Butter Cake

¼ lb. butter and 1 cup sugar, cream until smooth
2 eggs separated, add one yolk at a time, and mix between to butter mixture, add 1 cup milk and 1Tsp vanilla, Then 2 cups flour and 3 Tsp baking powder.
Fold in beaten egg whites. Bake 25-30 minutes at 350°

Chopped Apple Cake

2 Eggs, beaten
2 Cup sugar
1½ cup Wesson or Crisco Oil
2 t. vanilla
3 cups dried apples

Combine 3 cups all-purpose flour with 1 teas salt, soda, and cinnamon. Mix all ingredients to form stiff batter. Nuts can be added if desired (⅓ cup chopped) Bake in moderate oven 30-40 minutes.

Date Nut Pudding

1 cup boiling water
1 cup chopped date
1 cup sugar
1 tsp soda
1½ cup flour
1 tsp baking powd
1 tsp sugar
1 tsp butter
1 egg beaten

Pour water over dates; add soda and let sit until cool. Add sugar, butter and egg. Mix thoroly, sift flour and BP and add to mixture. Pour into greased 9x9 pan. Bake 350° until firm 35-55 minutes while cake is cooling make topping

1 cup chopped date
½ cup sugar
⅔ cup boiling water
Cook til thick, add ½ cup chopped nuts (walnuts or pecans?) Pour over cooled cake and spread. I serve with whipped cream or whipped topping.

Dump Cake

1 large can crushed pineapple
1 can cherry pie filling
1 pkg yellow cake mix
1 stick butter
½ cup nuts

Dump undrained pineapple and cherry filling in into 9x13 baking pan. Sprinkle dry cake mix on top; add nuts, dot with butter. Bake 45 minutes to 1 hour at 350°

Top with plain vanilla ice cream or cool whip. Store in fridge.

No Bake Fruit cake

1 lb. salted nuts
1 lb. pitted dates
½ cup candied cherries
½ cup candied pineapple
1 can sweetened condensed milk
½ lb., graham cracker crumbs

Mix all ingredients thoroughly, shape into desired cake pan. Place in refrigerator overnight. The longer it sits the better it tastes.

Zucchini Cake (she credits her sister Leni)

½ cup Oleo,
½ c. oil
½ teas gr. cinnamon and clove
2 cup shredded zucchini
1 cup nuts
1¾ cup sugar
2 eggs
1 t. vanilla
½ cup sour milk
2½ cup flour
4 T cocoa
½ t salt

Cream oleo, oil and sugar, add eggs, vanilla, milk-beat well, sift dry ingred., and add to mix beat well. Stir in zucchini and nuts, pour into 9x12x2 pan, and sprinkle ½ cup choc chips on top. Bake 325° for 1 hour. Very Good Recipe written on card

Cookie

Brownie Drops

2 pkgs 4 oz each Baker's German Sweet Chocolate
1 TBS butter
2 eggs
¾ cup sugar
¼ cup sifted flour
¼ teas baking powder
¼ tea cinnamon
⅛ teas salt
¾ cup pecans

Melt chocolate and butter over hot water, Stir and cool, Beat eggs until foamy, add sugar 2 T at a time, Beat til thicken (5 minutes on electric mixer) Blend in choc, flour, b.powder, and salt, Stir in nuts and vanilla, Drop by teaspoon, on greased cookie sheet, bake at 350° for 8-10 minutes

Cathedral Cookie

Melt together: 1 cup or 6 oz. choc.chips, 2 T butter or marg, cool
Add 1 beaten egg, and stir til smooth.
Mix together 3 cups colored miniature marshmallows, and ½ cup finely chopped nuts. Add cooked chocolate mixture and mix well. Spread finely cut coconut on waxed paper, Pour choc/marshmallow mixture on top. Form into long roll and freeze, cut into slices when serving.

Ice Box Cookie

1 cup brown sugar, 1 cup white Sugar,1 cup shortening
2 teas soda
4 cup flour
1 cup nuts
3 eggs
1 tbsp cinnamon
1 cup chopped dates

Mix like cookies, roll into logs in wax paper, chill overnight, slice and bake like cookies.

Lace Cookies

1 ½ cup brown sugar
2 TBS water
¼ cup butter
1 tsp cinnamon
1 cup finely chopped nuts (pecans)
1 cup flour

Mix sugar and water till thick paste, Cream butter and add paste, add rest of ingredients, dough like putty. Shape into <u>small</u> balls. Place on well greased cookie sheet, leave lots of room to spread. 350° for 10-15 minutes.

Marshmallow Balls

6 Heath bars (12 pieces) crushed into small pieces
1-14 oz sweetened condensed milk
¼ cup butter
48 large marshmallows
1 cup rice cereal, crushed coarsely

In a saucepan combine, toffee bars, milk and butter. Cook over medium heat 20-25 minutes til toffee is melted. Dip marshmallows into toffee mixture to cover marshmallow, roll in rice cereal. Dry on wax paper.

Peacan Pie Cookies

Pie Filing: ½ cup pd sugar, ¼ cup oleo, 3 TBS dark corn syrup, ½ cup chopped pecans. Combine sugar, oleo and corn syrup in pan, stir and cook over medium heat stirring often until a full boil. Remove from heat, stir in nuts and chill
1 c. oleo
½ cup sugar
½ dark corn syrup
2 eggs separated
2 ½ cup flour

Mix oleo and sugar, then add syrup and egg yolks, beat til blended, stir in flour and chill several hours. Shape in 1 to 1 ½ inch balls and place in muffin cups (can use small muffin tins) put indention in each cup. Bake for 7-10 minutes until set. While warm reshape the center of cookie to make well. Add 1 tablespoon of pie filling and bake 8-10 minutes Cool in pan for 10 minutes. Run a knife around the edges to loosen and then cool completely.

Quick Cookies

1 pkg semi sweet Choc. Chips
1 pkg butterscotch chips

Melt together over hot water, stir and remove from heat. Add 1-package cashews (whole) nuts, and 1 pkg Chinese noodles. Drop on cookie sheet by teaspoon. Put in refridge until choc. Is hard, does not need to be refrigerated, put in airtight container. Can use walnuts, peanuts, or almonds in place of cashews.

Peanut Butter and Coconut cookies

½ cup butter or Oleo
½ cup chunk peanut butter
1 c. brown sugar
1 egg
½ tsp each salt & vanilla
1¼ cup flour
¾ tsp baking soda
⅜ tsp baking powder
1 c moist flaked coconut

In large bowl, beat butter and peanut until blended. Add sugar, beat well. Then add egg, salt and vanilla. Separately, stir together, flour, baking soda and baking powder. Then stir in into butter mixture. Stir in coconut. On floured surface roll in into 2-1½ inch rolls. Wrap in wax paper. Chill two hours, slice in ³⁄₁₆ thick slices, and place 1½ inches apart on cookie sheet. Bake in preheated 350° oven for 8-10 minutes until golden brown. Remove to racks, and cool, Bakes 84 cookies

Oatmeal Choc. Chip Cookies

½ c. oleo
6 T brown sugar
¾ tsp. vanilla
1 cup oatmeal
1 egg
¾ c. flour
½ tsp each salt and soda
1-6oz choc chips

Cream and Mix, Drop by teaspoonful on greased cookie sheets, bake at 375° for 10 mins. About 3 doz.

Grandma Theresa in one of her many sweatshirts

Toffee Squares

1 cup shortening
1 cup brown sugar
1 egg
1 tsp. vanilla
2 cups flours
6 oz pkg. chocolate chip
½ cup chopped nuts

Cr. Shortening and sugar, Beat in Egg and vanilla, Mix in flour. Press into 10x15 pan. Bake at 350° for 18 minutes. While baking melt ch. Chips and spread over surface while hot, Sprinkle with chopped nuts. Cut into bars.

Zucchini Cookies

2 C flour
1 tsp Soda & B. Powder
1 tsp Cinn ¼ tsp Salt sift together
add dry Ing. to 1 cup sugar
½ c Crisco oil 1½ c grated Zucchini
Mix together add ½ c Raisins
½ c. nuts add butter flavoring
Bake 375 - 8-10 min
ungreased Cookie sheet - Frost.

Zucchini Cookies

2 cups flour
1 tsp baking soda and powder
1 tsp cinnamon
¼ tsp salt
Sift above together
Add dry ingredients to:
1 cup sugar
½ cup Crisco oil
1½ cup shredded zucchini
Mix together with
½ cup raisins
½ c. nuts
and butter flavoring

Bake at 375° for 8-10 minutes ungreased cookie sheet. Frost (no info on frosting)

Candies, Dessert and other Treats

Cherry Mash Candy

Combine 2 cups sugar with 16 regular marshmallows, and small can of evaporated milk, bring to a boil, boil for 5 minutes, and add 1 tea vanilla and 10 oz. package cherry chips, Mix well and pour in into 9x13 pan. Melt 12 oz. package chocolate chips. ¾ cup peanut butter, and 1 lb. salted chopped peanuts. Mix well and put on top of cherry mixture. Keep cool and cut into squares. Tastes like old fashioned Cherry mash.

Carmel Corn

8qt. popped Corn (unsalted & Hulless)
Mix together in saucepan
2 C. brown Sugar
3/4 C butter or oleo
1/2 C white Karo
1 tsp. Salt
Boil 5 Min, stirring often.
Add 1 tsp vanilla and 1 tsp Soda
over

Carmel Corn

8 Qt popped corn (unsalted and hulless)
Mix in saucepan,
2 cups brown sugar
¾-cup butter or oleo
½-cup white Karo
1 tsp salt

Boil 5 minutes, stirring often, add 1 tsp of vanilla and 1 tsp soda, after removing from heat, pour over popcorn in large roasting pan. Put into 250° for 1 hour, stirring every 10 to 15 minutes

English Toffee

1½ cup almonds, toasted in oven. Then rough chopped half, and split rest into halves.
¾ cup butter or substitute
¼ tsp salt
5 tsp. water
Milk chocolate, melted

Melt butter; add sugar, salt, and water, stirring until sugar dissolves. Cook to hard crack stage 310°F, stirring constantly. Add split almonds and pour into a greased pan 7¾ x 4* Pour ½ choc over top and sprinkle with ½ ch. nuts. When cool turn pan upside down on wax paper. Spread rest of choc and nuts. When cold break into pieces of desired size.

* pan size is loaf pan, but I remember these being made with cookie sheet with edge?

THE FUDGES

Divinity Fudge

3 cups Sugar
1 cup Karo Red Label
1 cup water
2 egg whites
1 tsp. vanilla
¼ salt
¾ cup chopped mixed nuts, dates, figs, or raisins

Combine karo, water, salt and sugar, boil until a little is tried In cold water is brittle (300°). Beat egg whites stiff, gradually beat in boiling syrup. Whip until it begins to stiffen, add vanilla, and fruit or nuts. Beat more and pour into slightly oiled pan or drop by teaspoonful. When cool, cut into squares.

Never Fail Fudge

4 cups sugar
1 lg can milk
1 cup oleo
12 oz chocolate chips
1 pt. marshmallow cream
1 cup walnuts

Cook first 3 ingredients until soft boil stage. Remove from heat, add remaining ingredients. Pour into a greased 9x13x2 pan. Set one hour before cutting.

Fudge Oatmeal

2 c sugar
½ c milk
½ c butter or margarine
Mix and let come to a boil
Pour over
3 c rolled oats
½ cup coconut, ½ cup cocoa ½ cup chopped nuts
1 tsp. Vanilla

Mix well, drop on wax paper by teaspoon. Keep in refridge in covered tight container.

Honey Rhubarb Betty

About 4 cups rhubarb, sliced
¾ cup sugar
1 tsp. Nutmeg
dash salt
2 T Water
6 T butter or oleo melted
½ cup honey
5 slice bread cut into cubes (about 4 cups)

Combine rhubarb and sugar, nutmeg, salt and water in a 10x6x1½ baking and dish, Spoon evenly, Blend butter and honey, Stir in bread cubes and spoon evenly over rhubarb mixture. Bake at 375° for 30 minute or until topping is light golden brown. Serve with cream.

Ice Cream

6 eggs
2¾ cups sugar
2 quarts milk (approx.)
1 Qt. whipping cream
2 T Vanilla
1 tsp. salt

Beat eggs, until light, add sugar a bit at a time. Beat in good. Add 1 ½ cup milk, cream, vanilla and salt, and mix well. Pour in freezer container, put into paddle, and if it does not reach the mark, add more milk to that point. Follow freezing directions

Popcorn Balls

2 cups sugar
2 T. light corn syrup
1⅓ cup water
½ tsp salt
2 tbs butter
vanilla or other flavoring
2 ½ qts unsalted popcorn

Combine sugar, corn syrup, water and salt, Put over low heat, a stir until boiling. Cook without stirring until it reaches 190° degrees. Add butter and flavor, but only stir enough to blend. Pour over corn in large mixing bowl. With hands that are well greased form into balls.

Ma's Shortcake*

1 heaping teas of butter
½ c sugar
½ c milk
2 eggs (separated)
1 cup cake flour
1 tsp. baking powder
1 tsp. vanilla

Cream sugar and butter, add beaten egg yolks, then milk. Alternate sifted flour and baking powder. Pour into greased and floured round cake tin. Beat egg whites stiff and add ½ cup sugar. Spread on top of cake batter. Bake at 350° for 25 minutes.

*written on bottom, my mom's recipe

Pecan Pie

3 eggs
1 cup dark karo
½ cup sugar
¼ oleo melted
1 tsp vanilla
1 cup pecans
1-9" pie shell

Heat oven to 350°, Beat eggs well, beat in syrup, sugar, oleo and vanilla until blended arrange pecans on bottom of pie crust, gently pour in mix. Bake 1 hour.

Family Photos

Raymond, Larry and Judith King. (1946 or 1947)

Judy King and parents

Larry and Roberta (Birdie)

Stacy, Amy, and Teri Watkins with Grandma Theresa at Christmas

I love that they were holding hands

Easter 1982(ish)

Jello Cakes, Desserts and Salad

Angel Delight

1 cup Sugar
½ cup Water
½ box Knox Gelatin
½ cup water
4 Egg Whites

Mix sugar and ½ cup water, boil about 15 minutes, Combine Knox and ½ cup water and set aside while syrup is cooking. Blend egg whites until stiff, add gelatin mixture to syrup and stir until dissolved slowly. Pour syrup into beaten egg whites, beating all the time. Continue beating until mixture thickens, add 1 tsp vanilla. Pour into 8x8 square baking dish and put into refridge overnight. When ready to serve, cut into squares, roll into graham cracker crumbs. Top with whipped cream.

Easy Rhubarb Cake

4 cups chopped Rhubarb
1 cup sugar
1 3 oz package strawberry Jello
1 cup mini marshmallow
1 white cake mix plus ingredients from pkg.

Placed rhubarb on bottom of greased cake pan, sprinkle with sugar and dry Jello, add layer of Marshmallows. Mix cake mix per directions, pour over and bake on lower rack in oven at 350° for 1 hour.

Molded Asparagus Salad

1 8 oz cream cheese
1 can asparagus soup
3 oz pkg, lime Jello

Heat soup, cheese and Jello with ¼ cup water, stir and smooth. Add ½ cup salad dressing, ¾ cup chopped celery, ½ cup chopped green pepper, ½ cup pecans. Pour into mold and refrigerator.

Lemon Chiffon Pie

1 TBS Knox unflavored Gelatins
¼ cup water
1 cup sugar
4 eggs (separated)
½ cup lemon juice
½ tsp salt
1 Baked pie shell

Soak gelatin in water. Beat egg yolks, until light, add ½ cup sugar, and lemon juice, continue to beat, when very light, place over low heat, cook stirring a custard consistency, Add gelatin and stir until dissolved. Cool. Beat egg whites and gradually add remaining sugar ½ cup at a time, beating til light and shiny. Fold egg yolk mix into whites, mix and pour into pie shell. Chill. Serve with thin layer of cool whip.

Peach Crisp (this might be Roberta King's recipe)

1 pkg inst. Van pud
1 cup sour cream
1 cup milk
Beat ingredients together
Fold in 1 cup sliced peaches. Chill
Topping
1 cup sugar, 1 beaten egg, 1cup walnuts

Mix and spread on greased tinfoil covered cookie sheet. Bake 350° 18-20 mins cool and break into pieces

Serve pudding with broken up crisp.

Pistachio Squares (clipping from newspaper)

1 cup flour
½ cup margarine
⅔ cup plus 2 tablespoon confectioners' sugar
½ cup cashew nuts
1 8 oz cream cheese
1 large carton whip topping, thawed
2 pkgs instant pistachio pudding mix
2 ½ cup milk
Cherries

Mix, flour, marg and 2 TB sugar and nuts. Press into lightly greased 9x13 pan, and bake at 350° for 15 minutes and cool.

Mix the cream cheese, ⅔ cup confectioner sugar, and ½ whip topping and spread on first layer. Beat together instant pudding and milk, spread on second layer, Spread remaining whip topping op top, place cherry in each piece, refrigerate, cut into squares

Raspberry Salad

1 pkg. raspberry Jello
1 cup applesauce
10 oz of fresh raspberry

Follow Jello package recipe. After mixing, add rest of ingredients and chill until firm before serving.

Tangy Lemon Sherbet

¾ cup white sugar
1½ tsp. unflavored gelatin
¼ cup lemon juice
1 tsp. grated lemon rind
1 egg white, stiffly beaten

Blend sugar, and gelatin in saucepan, and water, stir over low heat until gelatin dissolves. Cool, add juice and rind. Pour into metal freezer tray and freeze until a mush. Fold beaten egg whites into mixture, freeze until firm. Stirring occasionally, serve in sherbet glasses 4-5 servings.

Strawberry Cake

1 white cake mix
¼ cup salad oil
½ package frozen sliced strawberries
1 pkg. stawberrry gelatin
4 eggs
½ cup water

Combine all and beat with mixer 4-5 minutes, Bake according to package

Icing:

1 pkg powdered sugar
¼ lb. soft butter
½ pkg, frozen strawberries
Combine and beat with mixer until light and fluffy, Put on cold cake

Waldorf Salad

1 pkg lemon Jello
1 cup hot water
1 cup cold water

Mix per package directions. Add ½ mix in mold. Mix ½ cup Mayo, ⅛ salt, ½ celery, 1½ cups chopped, unpeeled apples, ¼ cup nuts. Mix with rest of Jello. Top the rest of the mix on plain Jello. Chil then Serve with whipped topping.

Watergate *Cover up Cake* Cake

1 white cake mix
3 egg whites
3/4 c. oil
1 c. seven 7-Warm
1 pk. pist pudding Mix according
to recipe - Slowly add 7 up
    13 x 9   ''   Bake 30 to 35
           ''
       Frosting
1 pk. Pudding
2 - Dream whip
1 1/2 c milk
         ''

Frost cake & refrigerate.

Meats

Barbeque Spareribs

3# spareribs
1 medium Onion
2 Tbs Vinegar
2 " br. Sugar
2 " lemon juice
1 tsp, salt
1 cup ketchup
2 Tbs Worchester
½ t horseradish or mustard
½ cup ch. celery
¾ cup Water

Brown ribs in deep skillet, remove ribs from pan, add butter, add sliced onion, and cook slowly til browned, add ribs and cook 20 mins. Mix other ingredients well and pour sauce over ribs and bake in oven for 1 hour or until ribs are tender.

Barbecue Beef

1 ½ cup beef cubes (1 inch)
2 T sugar
1 can beef Broth
½ cup water
¼ cup ketchup
1 T mustard (prepared)
1 clove garlic
dash tabasco sauce
2 large onions (quartered)
1 small gr. pepper, cut up
1 ½ cup. Sliced mushrooms
2 T flour

In skillet brown beef in shortening, pour off fat, add soup, ¼ cup water, ketchup, mustard, garlic, T sauce, and seasonings, Cook 1 ½ hrs, add onions. Cook 40min more, add rest of vegetables, cook 20 min. longer til tender, Blend ¼ cup water, with flour until smooth, slowly stir into stew, cook and stir till thickened. 6 servings.

Chicken Stew

Brown cut up chicken, remove from pan, add 2 T butters, and brown 2 cup cut onions, Pour 1 cup vermouth and 1 cup broth, Add chicken back to pan, sprinkle with Oregano, Add thick slices of potatoes. Cover simmer for 30 minutes.

Chicken and Yogurt

8 chicken thighs (or 4 chicken breasts) rinse and skinned
1 cup plain Yogurt
1 tsp paprika
1 tsp ginger
1 tsp cumin
salt and pepper to taste
3 garlic cloves crushed
2 T lime juice

Marinate chicken in yogurt, spices and juice overnight. Bake at 350° til done, serve with Saffron Rice

Saffron Rice

2 cups Rice
1 Tsp Saffron
4 cup cold beef broth
1 tsp. beef extract
2 cups parmesean cheese
½ cup Butter

Put Rice and Saffron in pan, add beef broth and bring to Boil. Reduce and simmer 10-15 minutes. Add butter and cheese, mix and serve.

Fish Fry Mix

1 cup white flour
1 cup yellow corn meal
1 TBS baking powder
1 egg
salt and pepper
1 can beer (about)

Mix, dip fish into batter and fry in ¾ deep fat. (works well on white fish)

Christmas 1986

Hawaiian Supper

Sauté 2½ cups slivered ham and ½ cups chopped green pepper in 2 TBS of butter until lightly browned.

Combine 1⅓ cups pineapple juice and water equal parts, with 2 to 4 TBS vinegar, 2 TBS each brown sugar and corn starch, ½ tsp each dry mustard and salt. Mix well, add to ham, and cook until thickened and transparent, stirring constantly. Add in ⅓ cups pineapple chunks which you have already drained and used in the sauce.

In saucepan, combine 1 ⅓ cup hot water, 1 tsp salt, dash of pepper, 2 TB chopped green onion and ⅓ cup minute rice. Stir. Pour into center of sauce and ham mixture. Bring to boil, cover and simmer for 5 minutes until rice is fluffy. Serves 4. Good Luck.

Ham Loaf and Cherry Sauce

Get1 ½ ham loaf meat from butcher, Mix ¼ cup milk, 1 cup soft bread crumbs, 1 beaten egg, ½ teas dry mustard, Mix into hamloaf, pack into bread loaf pan or form into loaf shape and spread 1 teas mustard, ½ cup brown sugar over the top. Bake at 350° for 1 ¼ hrs. Serve with the following 1 no. 2 can red sour cherries, 2 TBS corn starch, ½ cup sugar. Mix in saucepan and cook stirring until thick.

Stuffed Cabbage Leaves

12 large cabbage leaves
¾# gr. Veal
¾ # gr. Beef
4 T grated onion
½ cup butter
1½ cup cooked rice
2 TBS chop. fresh dill
1 tsp. thyne
3 cup canned tomato sauce
1 tsp salt
fresh gr. Pepper

Combine meats and sauté with onion in butter til brown, Add rice, dill, thyme salt and pepper and mix well.

Put cabbage leaves in salted boiling water for one minute. Drain and pat dry. Spoon meat mix on center of the leaves, fold over envelope style and secure with a toothpix, place in a greased shallow pan, pour tomatoe sauce over, cover and bake at 325° for 45 minutes.

Salami

2# Hamburger or ground pork
2 T Tenderizer
salt
1tsp liquid smoke
½ tea garlic salt, 2/2 pepper
1 cup water

Mix thoro, let stand overnight in refridge. Shape tightly into rolls in alum foil.Put on cookie sheet, Bake at 350° for 1 ½ hour, chill and slice. Keep in fridge.

Red Beans and Pasta

Several cloves garlic sliced, add to pan with butter, gently brown, but watch closely as it will burn fast. Add one can partially drained red beans (not chili beans) when heated through toss with hot rigatoni pasta. Sprinkle good parm. Cheese on top

*this recipe got me through college testing and late night studying.

Zucchini Beef Casserole

2# slices zucchini, sliced length wise,
1 ½ lean hamburger
1 chopped onion
1 cup rice (raw)
1-4 oz. chopped green chilies
2 T parm. cheese
1 tsp salt, ¼ tsp pepper
¼ t garlic powders
1 ½ cottage cheese
2 eggs beaten,
2 C, grated cheese, separated in 1 cup containers

Cook Zucchini in salted water 5 minutes and set aside, sauté meat, onion and seasonings and set aside, In big bowl blend eggs and cottage cheese, mix all ingredients together, with 1 cup of cheese and put all into 2 greased 2 quart casserole pans, top with ½ cup of remaining cheese on each casserole. Bake 350° about 30 minutes or until bubbly. Each casserole 6 each.

Grandma Theresa Classics

Pasties

1 lb round steak, cut off fat and cube
2 large potatoes, peel and cube
1 med. onion, cubed
salt and pepper to taste

Follow recipe for pie crust dough. Mix meat, onions and seasonings. Place portions on the dough, dot with butter, fold over and seal edges. Bake at 350° for 45 minutes.

Homemade Noodles

1 beaten egg
½ tea salt
2 Tbs milk
1 cup flour

Mix and roll thin. Let stand at least 1 hour, cut into strips and boil until done.

Spanish Sauce for Eggs

3 ripe tomatoes, seeded
clove garlic
1 small yellow onion
green peppers
salt pepper and dash of tabasco

Mince garlic, rough chop rest of vegetable. Put in heavy pan, bring to light boil then turn down heat and cook 1-2 hours until thick. Serve with eggs.

Fried Zucchini

3 medium zucchini
pepper and flour
2 egg plus 2 TBS milk
fine soda cracker crumbs

Cut zucchini in thirds, and then each third in ½ in strips. Dip into seasoned flour, then egg and milk mix, and crumbs. Let stand. Cook in hot oil 375° until light brown.

*I remember crushing the crackers by rolling a can of soup over a bag of crackers before I was in grade school.

Bagna Cauda

2 cup olive oil
8-10 cloves garlic, peeled and rough chopped
12 anchovy fillet in oil
½ cup dry red wine
4 T unsalted butter
8 cups cut up vegetables like carrots, spring onions, endives, bell peppers, Jerusalem artichokes, broccoli, and cauliflowers
2-3 cups fresh lean meats, sliced thin, (beef or pork are traditional, but chicken will work but cut in cubes)
2-3 loaves good spongy bread or crusty bread. Torn into pieces.

Rinse anchovies, then, debone the anchovies and discard the fins. Finally, soak the anchovy's fillets into red wine for 1 hour. Put garlic in pan with one cup oil and heat slowly, At this point, place the pot over a medium/low flame. You want the garlic to be very gently simmering: it has to become tender but still white. Once the garlic is ready, crush it with a spoon, then raise the anchovies from the wine and add them into the pot. Keep crushing the anchovies and garlic, then add the other cup of oil and cook 10 minutes more stirring frequently. Once ready, transfer to a fondue pot with heat source or electric frying pan. Heat to bubbly; gently dip your vegetable or meat into garlic mixture and lightly fry individual pieces. Use your bread pieces as transport from hot oil to you plate, so you do not get hot oil on table. If you can, have one pot for veggies, and one for meat. Open windows and drink plenty of good red wine.

Kraut Runzas

Filling 1½# hamburger
1 onion, 1 med head cabbage
1 cube margarine
salt and pepper

Cook Hamburger, onion chopped, shredded cabbage, and margarine, cook until cabbage is tender, drain off juice. May be used hot or cold to fill

1 pkg Hot Roll Mix, mix and let rise, twice, divide dough in 6 equal parts, Roll each into 7x4 strips put 3-4 T filling in each, Pull dough around filling and seal.

Bake 350° until golden brown.

Fruit Cake Cookies

⅔ cup brown sugar
½ butter or Oleo
1 egg
1 teas Vanilla
1 cup flour
⅛ tea. Salt.
½ teas baking powder
1# dates
4 oz candied cherry halves
2 candied pineapple slices chopped
½ cup pecans chopped
½ cup whole filberts
½ cup walnuts, chopped

Cream sugar and oil til light and fluffy, add egg, vanilla, and beat well. Stir together flour, soda and salt add to creamed mixture beating until well combined, mix in fruit and nuts. Chill batter. Drop by TBS on greased cookie sheet. Bake 325° for 12 minutes. Store baked cookies overnight in airtight container to soft.

Waldorf Astoria Red Rose Cake

½ cup butter
1½ cup sugar
2 eggs
2 Tbs cocoa
2 oz red food coloring
1 tsp. vanilla
2¼ cupcake flour
1 tsp salt
1 tsp soda
1 cup buttermilk
1 Tbs vinegar

Cream sugar and butter with mixture, add eggs 1 at a time and beat well. Make a paste with cocoa, food coloring and vanilla. Add to mixture, Use mixer only up to this point to blend. Sift Flour, salt and soda, fold in alternately with one cup milk. And finally add vinegar. Bake in 2-9" layer pans with bottom lined with wax paper. 350° for 30 minutes

7 Minute Frosting (Bertie recipe)

2 egg whites
1½ cup sugar
1 ½ tea corn syrup
¼ tea cream of tartar
1/3 cup cold water
Dash salt
1 t vanilla

Place everything except vanilla, in double boiler, Beat 1 minute, cook over boiling water beating consistently for 7 minutes. Remove from heat. Add vanilla. Beat until spreading consistency.

Cinnamon Pie (She credits Della, who is Dick's brother Fred King's wife)

4 T sugar
2 level tsp. cinnamon
5 rounded T of flour
pinch salt

Mix together.

Add 1 ½ cup water + ½ cup milk slowly, Pour into a pie crust and dot with butter. Bake slowly. Della's comment… hope this thickens.

Drinks

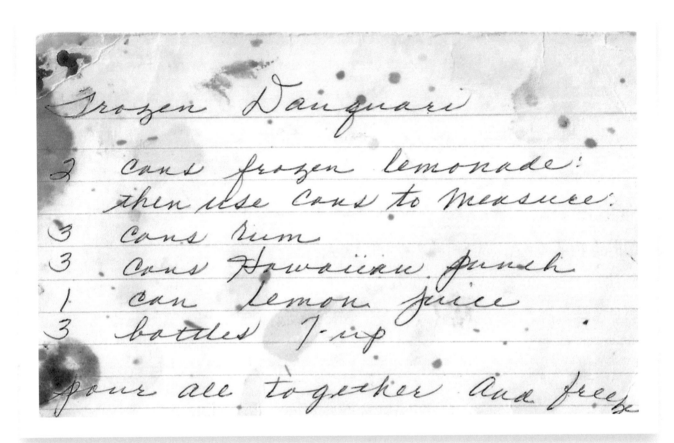

Frozen Daiquiri's

2 cans frozen lemonade, keep can to measure
3 cans Rum
2 cans Hawaiian Punch
1 can lemon juice
3 bottles 7-up

Mix and pour into plastic bowl, with tight cover, and freeze. It takes a couple days to freeze into a slush. Serve in stemmed cups with short straw.

Limoncello Punch (note on card: can be used for cocktails)

10 peels of 10 lemons, as much of the white pith removed, add to 1 bottle good vodka
Keep on the counter for at least 4 days

Cook 3½ cups water with 2½ cups Sugar to form a syrup let cool and then mix vodka with peels removed. Chill for minimum 4 hours, Put into punch bowl with 7 up, with fresh lemon slices

Berry Patch Punch

2 cans frozen raspberry lemon punch (she wrote in use raspberry lemonade)
2 cups water
1 pkg 10 oz, frozen raspberry
1 to 1½ cups bourbon
1 qt soda water

Empty punch, water and raspberries into bowl, let set 10-15 mins, Mix well, stir in bourbon and soda water. Serve over ice.

Kahlua

2 oz jar instant coffee
4 cups sugar
2 cups boiling water
1 vanilla bean cut up
1 pint of Brandy

Mix coffee with sugar and add to boiling water, take off stove, and vanilla bean, then brandy. Shake well and often while standing at rest for at least 30 days, The longer that it sits, it gets thicker.

Salads, Pickles and Relishes

5 Cup Salad

Combine
1 cup mandarin oranges slices
2 cups coconut
1 carton sour cream
1 cup drained crushed pineapple,
1 cup miniature marshmallows

Place in refridg, till thoroly chilled.

Cauliflower-Broccoli Salad

1 head broccoli
1 head cauliflower
1 small bunch green onions
1 cup mayo
1 cup sour cream
2 packs Hidden Valley Ranch Dressing

Chop vegetable into bites size pieces. Mix dressing and stir in. Refridge 3-4 hrs

Cauliflower Relish

½ head cauliflower, chopped small
¾ cup oil
2 tsp lemon juice
½ tsp salt
1/3 tsp dry mustard
1 cup cooked peas
2 oz canned mushrooms sliced

Mix together in bowl and chill. When serving add 2-3 bacon crumbles.

Chunky Coleslaw

1 package of cabbage 1#
4 green onions
1 pkg Ramona* noodles, broken up fine
3 oz slivered almonds
1/8 cup sesame seeds
¼ cup margarine

*I assume this is Ramen noodle, but it might have been a brand name

Mix together and chill before serving.

Cranberry Salsa

1# cranberries
1 cup sugar
1# Tokay* grapes
1 cup chopped nuts
1 pt wh. cream or pkg of dream whip.
1 chopped apple

*Tokay grapes were from California, They were sweet and had seeds. They are also used in sweet wines, but not as popular now as seedless grapes are the norm.

Grind cranberries and drain for 1 hour. Mix cranberries with sugar and let stand and for 1 hour- add grapes, apples and nuts. Fold cream in fruit, mix. Chill. Serves 12

Sweet and Sour Mushrooms

2-6 oz cans whole mushrooms
1T lemon juice
3 T Sugar
½ t Salt
¼ c. white vinegar
2 T water

Heat sugar, salt, vinegar, lemon juice and water to boiling point. Pour over mushrooms, cover and chill.

24 Hour Salad

2 eggs, beaten
4 T vinegar
4 T Sugar
2 T Butter
2 cups Royal Cherries, halved
2 cups tidbit pineapple
3 Oranges
1 cup whipped cream
2 cups miniature marshmallows*

Put eggs in dbl boiler; add vinegar and sugar, beating constantly until thick and smooth. Remove from heat, add butter and cool. When cold fold in whipped cream and fruit, turn into mold and refridg for 24 hours. Serves 12-14

*no mention of adding marshmallows in original recipe, so add them with fruit.

Sweet Zucchini pickles

1 ½ gal. sliced zucchini (not peeled)
¾ c salt
4 onions (sliced)
2 green peppers (chopped)
2 can red pimentos

Arrange in layers with salt, the above ingredients, cover with two trays of ice and let stand 3 hrs and then drain.

Syrup:
1 ½ cup sugar
¼ t cloves
2 t mustard seed
1 ½ t turmeric
1 t celery seed
2 cloves garlic (chopped)
3 ½ cup vinegar

Bring to a boil add zucchini and cook til tender.

Whole Green Tomatoe Pickles

8 lbs small green tomatoes
½ cup salt
1 pint water
1 pint white vinegar
3 lbs sugar
12 whole cloves
4 sticks cinnamon

Peel tomatoes and let stand overnight, Next morning, dry, and then cover with water and ¼ cup salt. Bring to boil and boil 5 minutes, drain and set aside. Boil pints of water, vinegar, sugar, cloves and cinnamon. As soon as this becomes a syrup, add tomatoes, and boil a minute or two longer. Pour into crock and let stand for 3 days. Reheat again. Put tomatoes into jars; pour in hot syrup and seal. *no mention about hot water bath canning.

Vegetables and Soups

Gazpacho Soup

1 cucumber, peeled and seeded
½ red onion
5 tomatoes peeled and seeded
1 tsp. salt in ¼ cup hot water
¼ cup red wine vinegar
2 cloves garlic
1 tsp paprika
½ tsp tabasco sauce
24 oz tomato juice
salt and pepper

Dice all veggies, mix with all ingredients, and chill. Serve cold with sour cream.

Fluffy Light Skillet Corn Fritters

1 egg
1 cup milk
1 cup pancake mix
1-120 oz whole corn kernels, drained

Wesson oil to depth of one inch.

Blend egg and milk, add pancake mix, and stir until fairly smooth (batter will be stiff). Fold in corn, Drop by tsps. Into hot Wesson oil. Cook quickly until golden brown, about 4 minutes. Makes 24. Pour on log cabin syrup.

Golden Maple Corn

Beat 4 eggs til foamy. Add ½ cup maple syrup. Melt and add ¼# Butter. Beat well. Put 2-10 oz packages of frozen corn in greased baking dish, slowly pour egg mixture into dish. Bake 1 hour or till crusty. Brown in 350° oven Stir just once. serves 6

Photo by Cherri Dupree

Teri Watkins is the oldest child of Judy, Theresa's only daughter, and shares Theresa's first name. During elementary school breaks, she and her two sisters spent several weeks with their grandparents, and Teri spent time learning to cook and garden.

In high school, Teri's family moved to Lincoln, and she was able to spend more time with grandparents until she moved to Omaha after college.

Teri moved from Omaha, Nebraska, to Bloomington, Indiana, in 2000. She spends her time visiting state wineries with friends, cheering for the Indiana Women's basketball program, gardening, volunteering, and cooking. She works in publishing.

Richard King died in 1988. Theresa died ten years later in 1998.

Printed in the United States
by Baker & Taylor Publisher Services